JOHN TOWNSEND

Badger Publishing Limited
Oldmedow Road,
Hardwick Industrial Estate,
King's Lynn PE30 4JJ
Telephone: 01438 791037

www.badgerlearning.co.uk

4 6 8 10 9 7 5 3

Sharks ISBN 978-1-78147-539-3

Publisher: Susan Ross
Senior Editor: Danny Pearson
Designer: Fiona Grant

Photos: Cover image: REX/Design Pics Inc
Page 4: Design Pics Inc/REX
Page 5: Design Pics Inc/REX
Page 6: L Winburn/Newspix/REX
Page 7: Dan Callister/REX
Page 8: Universal History Archive/UN/REX
Page 10: US warship Indianapolis
Page 11: Design Pics Inc/REX
Page 13: Image Source/REX
Page 14: Cultura/REX
Page 17: Nature Picture Library/REX
Page 18: Tom Campbell/SplashdownDirec/REX
Page 19: Courtesy Everett Collection/REX
Page 22: Design Pics Inc/REX
Page 24: S Robertson/Newspix/REX
Page 25: Julien Chatelin/REX
Page 28: WestEnd61/REX
Page 29: Image Broker/REX
Page 31: F1 Online/REX

Attempts to contact all copyright holders have been made.
If any omitted would care to contact Badger Learning, we will be happy to make appropriate arrangements.

Contents

1. MAN-EATERS

The word 'shark' means one thing to many people – DANGER! Yet sharks are in more danger from humans than we are from them. We kill thousands every day.

Every year, sharks attack people – but not many. About ten people are killed by sharks in a year. Those deaths make the news. They make our blood run cold.

If you swim in Australia, South Africa or the USA, you might see some of these great creatures. They might see you, too. Would you risk swimming there?

Some sharks feed on seals near to the shore. A surf board can look just like a seal from below. That is when a shark will rise and bite with its rows of razor-sharp teeth. It will soon be over.

Bits of surf board and blood will drift away. All that will remain will be the screams from the beach...

WOW! facts

Many sharks have dark backs and pale bellies. (This makes them tricky to see from above and below!)

Early Escape

More people swim or surf now than ever before. That means there are likely to be more shark attacks. But sharks have been biting us for hundreds of years!

In 1749, 14-year-old Brook Watson went for a swim in the sea off Cuba. That's when a shark struck.

Brook's shipmates saw the shark attack. They pulled him from the water – just as his foot was bitten off. He later had to have his leg sawn off below the knee. Years later he was famous – not just for his lucky escape. He became the Lord Mayor of London.

In 1778, the artist John Singleton Copley painted a picture of Brook Watson's attack.

BIGGEST KILLERS

There are many sorts of shark – almost 500 species. Most of them are harmless to humans. The three types most likely to attack us are bull sharks, great white sharks and tiger sharks.

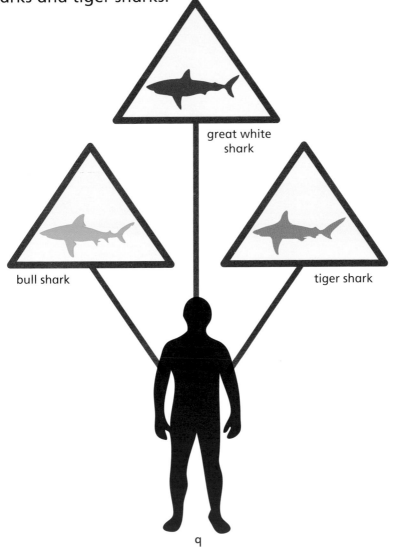

great white shark

bull shark

tiger shark

One of the worst shark attacks ever was during World War Two. In 1945, the US warship Indianapolis sank in the Pacific Ocean. About 900 American sailors jumped into the sea as the ship went down. The men wore life-vests and floated in the water all night.

At sunrise, the sharks arrived. The sailors were helpless against the hungry man-eaters. Some days later a seaplane landed to rescue the survivors. Only 317 men were rescued. It was the worst sea disaster in US Navy history. No one knew exactly how many sailors died from drowning or thirst ... and how many were victims of the dreaded sharks.

2. BULL SHARKS

Many experts say the most dangerous shark of all is the bull shark. That's because this shark can be very fierce and 'charge like a bull'. It even swims up rivers and has been known to crunch canoes in half! Bull sharks often hunt where people swim in shallow, warm water.

BULL SHARK FACTS

- They often live to about 16 years old.

- They can grow to between 2 and 3.5 metres long.

- They are also known by other names, such as Zambezi sharks and Ganges sharks. These are names of rivers where the sharks have killed people in small boats.

- They have wide heads with a short, blunt snout.

- They eat almost anything – using their rows of razor-sharp teeth (which they often leave stuck in the bones of victims).

WOW! facts

Bull sharks can live in salt water or fresh water. Some bull sharks have even attacked people in their own homes during floods! (Just when you thought it was safe to go back in the bathroom...)

OUT OF THE BLUE

South Africa – 1988

Belinda (15) and her friends went surfing before breakfast. She lay on her board with her head on her arms. It was good to feel the sun on her back and the warm sea below. She was almost asleep when a jolt spun the board and she fell into the water.

A large bull shark rushed up and bit into her leg three times. She screamed and hit out, thumping at the shark's face. It shook her in its jaws and tried to pull her under. Her friends rushed over – and the shark let go, taking a chunk of Belinda's leg with it.

Her friend pushed a fist into her leg to stop the bleeding. They pulled her onto the beach where they sent for help. They worked hard to stop her passing out and from seeing her leg.

A doctor came and fixed up a drip. She was rushed to hospital where she was given six pints of blood. Her leg had to be cut off just below the hip. Even so, she went home a few weeks later and lived to surf another day!

August 2013

BULL SHARK ATTACK!

A teenager is lucky to be alive after a bull shark attacked him while he was wading in Florida. He had the scare of his life while fishing near the shore.

"I've now got a hole in my leg and teeth marks," said 17-year-old Christian Mercurio. "I felt like I was being bitten so I just kicked whatever it was. It bit my left foot. I just ripped my leg out of the shark's mouth and started running."

Mercurio's mother wrapped up his leg and rushed him to hospital. He was lucky not to lose his foot. "I'm just really glad that I'm still alive and with my family," said Mercurio.

3. GREAT WHITE SHARKS

The great white shark is the most feared of all sharks. It is the largest of the man-eating sharks, with females being larger than the males. Some are as long as six metres and may weigh over 3,000kg.

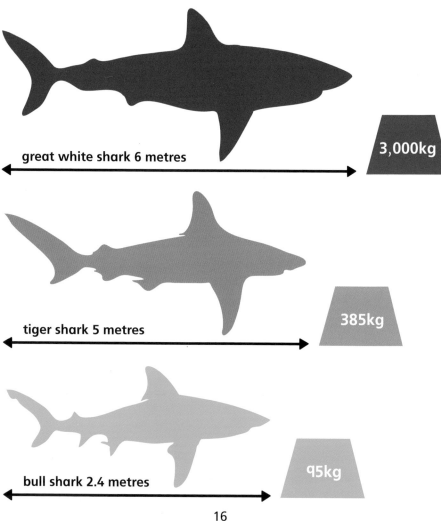

great white shark 6 metres

3,000kg

tiger shark 5 metres

385kg

bull shark 2.4 metres

95kg

Adult great white sharks can open their jaws over a metre wide. They push forward rows of teeth, each tooth being almost six centimetres long. The jaws slam shut with the force of three tons per square centimetre (like having three cars pressing down on the tip of one finger!).

Many years before the film *Jaws*, a real great white shark attack in California made world news. It brought fear to the golden beaches of America.

The terrifying motion picture from the terrifying No. 1 best seller.

JAWS

WOW! facts

Baby great whites are about 1.5 metres long when they are born. They have to fend for themselves straight away.

Famous Attack

One of the most famous great white shark attacks was over 50 years ago.

Rodney Fox was spear-fishing in Australia in 1963 when a great white grabbed him around his middle.

It swam off, dragging Rodney upside-down through the water. He tried to gouge the shark's eyes and jam his arm down its throat. It ripped the flesh from his arm with its razor teeth.

As the shark dragged him along the ocean floor, Rodney struggled free. He rose to the surface and was pulled into a boat.

His rescuers kept his wetsuit on to stop his organs spilling out of his wounds. Despite horrific injuries and after 360 stitches, Rodney lived to tell his tale.

He is the most famous shark survivor in Australia.

2013 – San Francisco, USA

LUCKY TO BE ALIVE!

Micah Flanaburg is lucky to be alive. He and his father-in-law were fishing in kayaks off Pacifica State Beach when a great white attacked.

"It came up straight under me … and the whole kayak lifted out of the water," Micah said. "As it grabbed hold of me, it started shaking the boat front to back. It wouldn't let go."

After it bit into the kayak, the shark circled the craft and swam away.

"The scariest part was when it let go. It swam back round and I thought it was going to come and take another bite, right where my legs were."

Flanaburg thought the great white shark was about four metres long. "I was pretty much helpless, just hanging on for dear life," he said.

Luckily the shark had second thoughts and swam off.

4. TIGER SHARKS

The tiger shark is another of the sharks most feared by surfers. It gets its name from its stripes, but also from the fierce way it fights. Some grow up to six metres long. It is second only to the great white shark for attacks on humans.

TIGER SHARK FACTS

- They swim and hunt alone.
- They swim at the surface and to a depth of 350 metres – in open sea or along the shore.
- They are found around the world in warm seas.
- They tend to swim at just two or three miles per hour ... with fast bursts before an attack.

WOULD YOU BELIEVE IT?

All sorts of things have been found in
the stomachs of tiger sharks.
How's this for a menu?

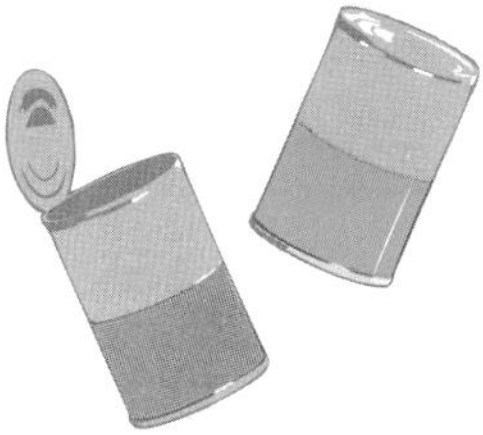

tin cans

part of a dog

human arm

shoes

small goat

lumps of coal

car number plate

bottles

YOU NAME IT, THEY'LL EAT IT!

TRUE STORY

Bethany Hamilton (aged 13) was Hawaii's top surfer for her age when terror struck in 2003.

A 4.5 metre tiger shark attacked when she went surfing one morning. She was lying on her board with her left arm dangling in the water when the shark came up from below. It bit her arm off just below the shoulder. Her surfing partners quickly tied a strap round her shoulder to stem the bleeding. She passed out on the beach while waiting for an ambulance.

Bethany Hamilton of Hanalei, Kauai, Hawaii

Although Bethany lost over half of her blood, doctors managed to save her. Within a month, she was back on her surf board! It was harder to balance with only one arm but soon she was competing again. In 2005, she won her first national title for surfing. A hungry shark wasn't going to stop her!

2013 – Hawaii

SECOND SHARK ATTACK IN FOUR DAYS!

A second shark attack in four days has forced two beaches to close.

A woman was bitten when she went for an early morning swim about ten metres from the shore in Maui. She managed to swim to shore to get help.

Just days before, Kiowa Gatewood was surfing nearby when he saw a tiger shark.

"I was on my board when all of a sudden I saw this shark come out of the water and grab my leg," the 19-year-old said. "I hit it with my left hand and it let go and turned round and swam away."

He needed surgery on his left knee and upper calf. "Sharks can bite hard," he said, but he added that he plans to surf again.

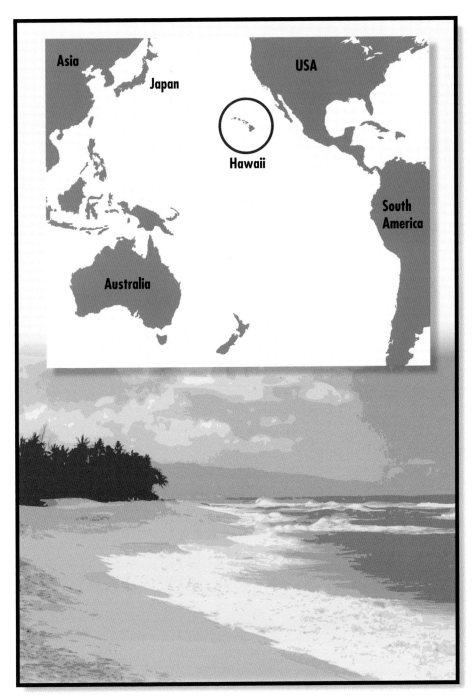

5. DID YOU KNOW?

How do sharks know when you go in for a swim?

Many sharks have special sensors on their heads. These can detect signals in the water. Anything swimming gives pulses of energy, which sharks sense from far away. Then they 'lock in' and zoom over to take a bite!

Sharks have very good hearing and a keen sense of smell. Sixty per cent of their brain is linked to the sense of smell. Sharks can smell blood in the water from several miles away.

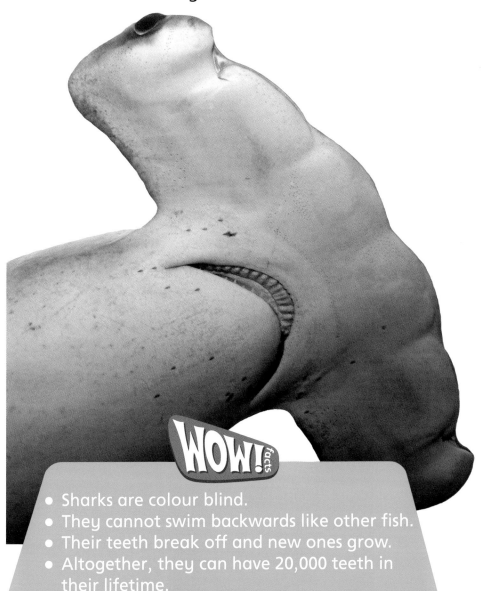

WOW! facts

- Sharks are colour blind.
- They cannot swim backwards like other fish.
- Their teeth break off and new ones grow.
- Altogether, they can have 20,000 teeth in their lifetime.

AND FINALLY

Just when you thought it was safe...

- Anyone who has swum in New Smyrna Beach, Florida (shark capital of the world), has probably been within three metres of a shark – and not even known!

- You have a 1 in 218 chance of dying from a fall and a 1 in 3.7 million chance of being killed by a shark.

- Ninety-three per cent of shark attacks from 1580 to 2010 worldwide were on males.

- A shark's liver is big and oily, and helps the shark float. Some sharks can live for a year without eating, surviving on the oil stored in their livers.

- For every one human killed by a shark, humans kill two million sharks. Even though sharks have been around for 350 million years, some species are now endangered.

INDEX